Bark at the Moon

THE OFFICIAL OSBOURNE PET BOOK

THE OSBOURNES WITH TODD GOLD

books™

MTV BOOKS / POCKET BOOKS

NEW YORK · LONDON · TORONTO · SYDNEY · SINGAPORE

An *Original* Publication of MTV Books/Pocket Books

POCKET BOOKS, a division of Simon & Schuster, Inc.
1230 Avenue of the Americas, New York, NY 10020

ISBN: 0-7434-7006-0

First MTV Books/Pocket Books trade paperback printing November 2002

10 9 8 7 6 5 4 3 2 1

POCKET and colophon are registered trademarks
of Simon & Schuster, Inc.

Cover design and interior design by Red Herring Design
All pet photographs by Christopher Ameruoso
Photo credits: Amy V. Cooper, pgs. 3, 8, and 18

Printed in the U.S.A.

For information regarding special discounts for bulk purchases,
please contact Simon & Schuster Special Sales
at 1-800-456-6798 or business@simonandschuster.com

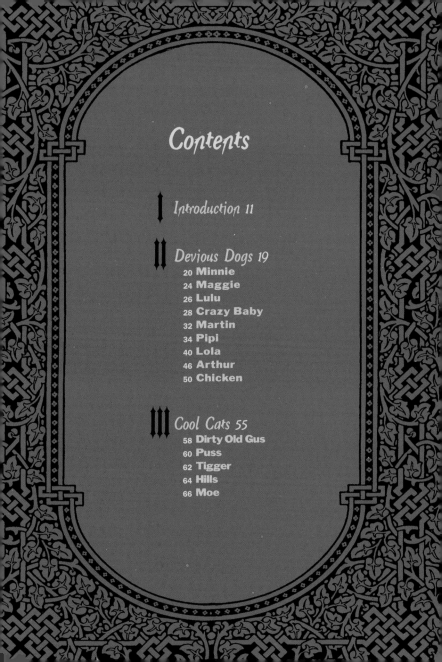

Contents

"I think we have a lot of pets
because we have a lot of love to share."
— Sharon Osbourne

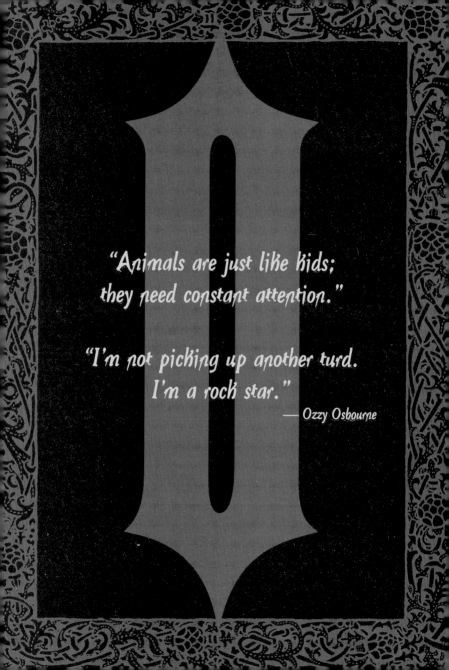

"Animals are just like kids;
they need constant attention."

"I'm not picking up another turd.
I'm a rock star."

— Ozzy Osbourne

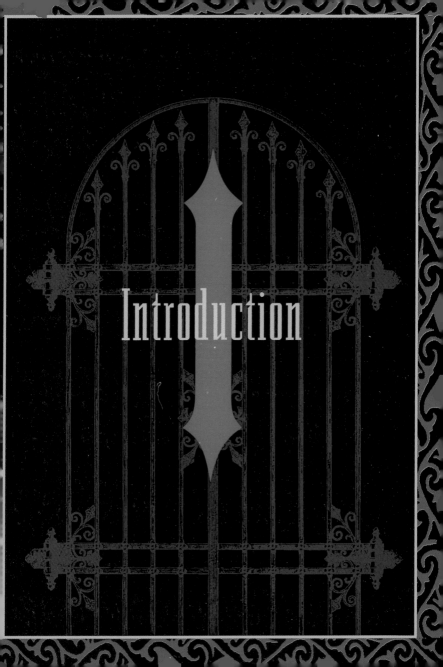

Introduction

EET THE OSBOURNES.
No, not Ozzy, Sharon, Aimee, Kelly, and Jack.
These Osbournes are the furry kind. They have
four legs. They sleep under the beds, not on
them. They eat out of bowls. They have had their
shots. They really do bark at the moon. And they are mostly house-
broken, but don't trust them with your sofas or rugs.

They are the family's "hair"-looms. They are dogs and cats. Their
names are Minnie, Maggie, Lulu, Crazy Baby, Martin, Pipi, Lola,
Arthur, Dirty Old Gus, Puss, Tigger, and Hills. They are the cutest,
naughtiest, and most lovable animals on MTV. And as Kelly says,
"They rock."

They aren't your run-of-the-mill, garden-variety pets. In terms of
dogs, they own Pomeranians, Japanese Chins, and Chihuahuas,
breeds known for their looks, loyalty, and temperaments. "They
are small but with enormous hearts," says Sharon. There's also
Lola, an uninhibited, playful bulldog. "She's just a great dog,"
says her owner, Jack. As for the cats, they have an Egyptian, an
Abyssinian, and a couple Rag Dolls. "I love 'em, sure, but I don't
understand why we have to have so many," says Ozzy.

"Sharon, why do we have to have so many #$&*ing dogs and
cats?" he asks.

"Oh darling, it's because God only made one of you," she says.

"No, really. I want an explanation."

"Because we have so much love to give. All of us do."

Spend any time at their home and you know that's true. Plus, Sharon is addicted to food, spending, *and* adorable little dogs and cats. And Ozzy is a pushover. Which doesn't mean he gets why their dogs continually soil their chairs, sofas, and carpets. "Why do they do it, Sharon?" he asked during the second episode of MTV's hit series, *The Osbournes*. "What's the deal?"

"They like pissing on #$&*ing antique rugs," said Sharon. "What can I tell you?"

None was worse than Lola.

"It's not like a little squirt," said Ozzy. "She must have a #$&*ing extra tank in her ass."

"What really pisses me off?" muses rock and roll's Prince of Darkness. "We've paid all this money to have this house renovated and the dogs...you might as well just live in a #$&*ing circus. The dogs piss everywhere."

Everywhere indeed. Though viewers of the series didn't ever see it, the dogs would wander into the two downstairs rooms that housed MTV's production crew and their equipment. "It was like a daily sniff," says *The Osbourne*'s executive producer, Greg Johnston. "They'd come in, check things out, hang around, and pee and #$&* just like they did in the rest of the house."

Did anyone complain? No. "Those animals provide us with an important life lesson," says Sharon. "Watch where you step." The great writer and director Nora Ephron once said, "You enter a certain amount of madness when you marry a person with pets." Similarly, you understand a certain amount of the Osbourne's craziness when you get to know their pets.

As Sharon says, "We're pet lovers. Doesn't that tell you something about us?"

"Did anybody feed the dogs today?"
—Sharon

"No, they can do without
a day of food."
—Kelly

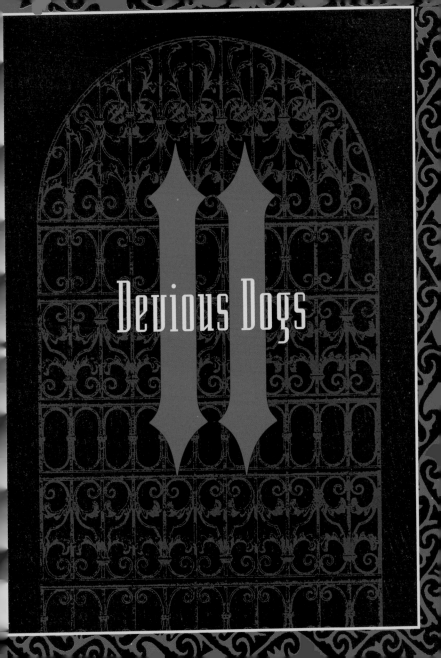

II

Devious Dogs

Minnie

AGE: 5
BREED: POMERANIAN
DISPOSITION: REGAL,
BITCHY, A STAR

"**M**innie is a bitch," says Kelly, "but she is the queen." No argument there. When she's with Sharon, she has the look of being in charge. And when she's not with Sharon? "That doesn't happen too often," says Melinda.

Minnie, 5, is one smart Pomeranian. She was originally Kelly's dog. "I bought her from a pet store in Malibu," says Kelly. "We had about a moment together. Then my mother got jealous and started hanging out with Minnie, who quickly decided she loved my mother and not me."

She can be moody and temperamental. "If I say 'hi' to one of the other dogs while Minnie's sitting there, she'll get upset," says Melinda. "If Sharon goes out without Minnie, she gets very annoyed and sits under the steps and won't come out until Sharon comes back."

She doesn't care. "Minnie's just an evil cow that loves all the attention," says Kelly.

It's true. Normally she doesn't have much patience for strangers, but Sharon and Osbourne publicist Lisa Vega were walking through New York's Central Park one day when people stopped them. Instead of asking for Sharon's autograph, they wanted to take photos with Minnie.

"Minnie loved it," says Lisa. "It was as if she was the one signing autographs."

She lives like a star. She spends all day with Sharon and sleeps under her's and Ozzy's bed at night. She also goes on virtually every road trip, providing various hotels with their own Minnie stories. Like the time she peed on the hallway rug at the Ritz–Carlton in Washington, D.C. as the Osbourne's were checking in at four A.M. "The hotel's VIP greeter showing us to our room was horrified," recalls Lisa. "Sharon ran into the room, got towels, and started mopping while I sprayed Chanel No. 5 on the spot. Then Sharon took a potted plant from the room and put it over the spot."

Sharon says Minnie's companionship more than makes up for such mishaps. "It's like when you're bonded with your best friend," she says. "I'm not happy when she's not with me and she's not happy when she's not with me."

For Sharon, Minnie's the perfect antidote for a bad day. "When I first got ill, she felt the atmosphere in the house," she says. "She just sat on my tummy for hours and wouldn't go."

MAGGIE

AGE: 5
BREED: JAPANESE CHIN
DISPOSITION: NICE, SHY, TOLERANT

Japanese Chin, she's the second dog the Osbourne's—actually Sharon—bought. The reason? "I didn't want Minnie to be lonely when I was out," says Sharon.

As far as the dogs go, Maggie is a good girl. For some reason, Sharon's brother calls her "the doctor." On the show, Sharon described her as "heroin chic." Translation: If Minnie is a rich bitch, Maggie is happy simply being rich.

She adores Ozzy and is shy around others. "She does have the sweetest disposition of all the dogs," says Kelly. "She's Melinda's favorite. But her breath always smells like fish."

If Ozzy's home, Maggie is usually laying at his feet. "She's the perfect balance for Minnie," says Sharon. "Minnie's kind of like me—very pushy, orders everyone around. Maggie's like Ozzy—gentle, funny, shy."

 She's also forgiving. "Yeah, Maggie takes all the #$&* that Minnie gives her," says Sharon. "She's like, 'Oh, Minnie, you're such a bitch. Go do something else.' And then she goes back to her business. They're a good pair."

Lulu

Age: 4
Breed: Chihuahua
Disposition: Docile, a survivor

riginally Kelly's dog, this black Chihuahua suffered a seizure when she was a puppy. She was rushed to the animal hospital, where the veterinarians and nurses worked feverishly to save her life. It seemed like a scene from an episode of *ER*. When the vet warned Sharon that Lulu probably wasn't going to make it, Kelly, then fourteen, cried, "Don't let her die!"

It wasn't up to them. For nearly a week, Lulu laid on a little hot water bottle in the pet hospital, her long tongue hanging out of her head. "She looked totally gone," says Sharon. "I mean, her eyes were in the back of her head, her breathing was shallow, and she didn't have enough energy to pull her tongue back in her mouth."

"But then one day," adds Kelly, "we arrived for a visit and Lulu was waiting on the little pillow we'd gotten her. Mom says she was waiting for me. In any case, she was ready to go home."

Since then, Lulu has been healthy, though the seizure left her slightly brain damaged. "She believes she's a pig," says Sharon. "She's very sweet and tame, but she woke up from her stroke thinking she was a pig. She grunts like a pig. I'm convinced she has no idea that she's a dog. But Lulu is a great one. She's a survivor."

CRAZY BABY

AGE: 3
BREED: JAPANESE CHIN
DISPOSITION: NUTS, SEX CRAZED

black–and–white Japanese Chin, as opposed to the brown–and–white Maggie, Crazy Baby is absolutely bonkers. "She's totally out of her mind," says Jack. "A freak."

At first, she was called New Baby, but then as the Osbournes realized she was neurotic, Sharon began calling her Crazy Baby. "Crazy Babies" was also the name of a song off of Ozzy's album <u>No Rest for the Wicked</u>. Soon the others picked up on it. The name fit her better. "She's got eyes like a lunatic," says Sharon, "and she's always got this mad grin on her face. Her tongue is always coming out."

"And she's a trouble maker," says Kelly.

Yes, Crazy Baby is constantly attacking the other dogs. Her favorite target is Lulu. She once bit Lulu's ear and refused to let go, dragging her across the kitchen until one of the kids pried her loose. Lulu's ear needed stitches, and now it flops rather than stands up. "That's when we started calling her Crazy Baby," says Sharon.

Perhaps it's hormonal. Among the Osbournes, there's a theory that Crazy Baby is a bit of a nymphomaniac. "She humps anything," explains Sharon. "Stuffed toys. Melinda. Anyone that comes in the house."

Including Ozzy and Sharon. "One night," says Sharon, "Ozzy and I were in bed and we were cuddling and messing around, and Crazy Baby jumped on Ozzy's back and started to hump him while he was on top of me. It was so weird. We looked at each other and said, 'Carry on.' Crazy Baby was going to do whatever she wanted. She's insane."

Martin

(AKA MARTINI BIANCO)

AGE: 2
BREED: CHIHUAHUA
DISPOSITION: ZOOLANDER

alk about loving. Talk about a gorgeous-looking dog. Talk about perfect markings. Talk about being gay. Then according to the Osbournes, you must be talking about their Chihuahua, Martini. "He's kind of like Zoolander," explains Sharon. "He knows he's hot, so he sits in these insanely egotistical, really quite stunning poses. He's like one of those guys from *Men in Black*. All he needs is a pair of shades."

But beware. "If you try to touch him," she adds, "Martin growls. He's like, '#$&* off, I'm voguing right now.'" "People come over and go, 'Hello, Martin, let me touch you and kiss you,' and he yelps," says Melinda. "It's embarrassing."

What about the gay thing? "He's seriously the gayest little bastard," she explains. "For example, if I go near him, he squeals like I'm going to torture him. On the other hand, he loves my husband. He loves all men."

"That's true," says Kelly, who is the only female Martin has any fondness for. "If there are ten girls in the room and one boy, he'll always go sit next to the boy. He won't let girls touch him unless he knows them. But he's cool."

Pipi

AGE: UNKNOWN
(PROBABLY 2 OR 3)
BREED: POMERANIAN (PROBABLY)
DISPOSITION: ENJOYS TRAVELING

From the day Sharon flew this almost pure–black Pomeranian to Beverly Hills from Florida as a birthday gift for Aimee, Pipi has wanted to get back on the road. "She's either the world's dumbest dog," says Sharon, "or she was once in a band and misses being on the road."

Regardless, Pipi shot to fame in spring 2002 when she slipped past security at the front gate and ran away from home. Past getaways had been thwarted by Michael, the security guard. But this time the Osbournes were out of town and she made it beyond the property, past the tour buses, and down the road without notice, thus beginning a long, strange journey.

Upset by her disappearance, the Osbournes figured she would turn up. Except this time was different. As it turned out, a neighbor found Pipi but didn't know who she belonged to. For some reason, she gave Pipi to her housekeeper, who took her home but wasn't able to keep her. The housekeeper gave Pipi to a friend living in Apple Valley, a small town about two hours outside of Beverly Hills.

But Pipi didn't stay put long. Within a few days, she ran away and was soon found by another Apple Valley do-gooder. That woman put an ad in a local newspaper saying she had found a cute Pomeranian. A woman who had coincidentally lost a black Pomeranian answered it.

But the dog wasn't hers. She knew it as soon as she saw Pipi. Yet the woman who had placed the ad couldn't keep Pipi because she was allergic. She asked if the woman wanted to keep Pipi anyway, otherwise she was taking her to the pound. Pipi then had her fourth home in a week.

Meanwhile, news of Pipi's disappearance had leaked out to the media. Sharon and Kelly were guesting on *Live with Regis and Kelly* in New York. During the show, they flashed a photo of Pipi and offered a $500 reward for anyone turning her in. Live's co-host Kelly Ripa got really involved, talked about it for days, and put up another $500.

Soon the media attention was worldwide. The Osbourne's publicist, Lisa, received inquiries from *Good Morning America*, the *Today* show, the *New York Post*, the London *Daily Mirror*, *People* magazine, and what seemed like every print and TV outlet from L.A. to England.

"It was torture for Aimee," says Melinda. "Pipi was her little baby. She was very upset. Then just as she was getting used the idea that Pipi was never coming home, the phone rang with good news."

Back in Apple Valley, the woman with Pipi was watching Regis and Kelly and thought the Pomeranian in her living room was the same one pictured on TV. By calling Sharon's office, she managed to get a hold of Aimee, who asked a few questions to make sure it was the right dog, including whether she was fixed.

"Yes, she is," answered the woman.

"Oops, that's not our dog," said Aimee.

But the next day the woman called back and said she'd made a mistake. The dog was fixed. Several hours later, they met and Aimee determined that it was indeed Pipi. Overjoyed, Aimee paid the woman the $1,000 reward money and added another $1,000 for good measure. Finally, to show their gratitude to Kelly Ripa, Sharon and her daughters sent the beautiful and compassionate TV co-host 100 yellow long-stemmed roses.

And Pipi? "She walked back in the house," says Melinda, "and I swear she had a look in her eyes that said, 'Oh #$&*, I'm back at this #$&*ing house again.'" At least Aimee's happy.

"They said Lola was beyond repair.
They said she was retarded.
Honestly, she's a fantastic dog."
— *professional dog trainer*
Tamar Geller

LOLA

AGE: 2
BREED: BULLDOG
DISPOSITION: BIG,
BOISTEROUS, ADORABLE

zzy was walking Lola along the beach in Malibu one day this past summer. As they strolled past a bunch of picnickers, Lola took off. Snatching someone's basket of food in her jaws, she ran down the beach, leaving Ozzy to apologize. "I guess she's back," said one of the picnickers. "Yes, the devil has returned," said Ozzy.

None of the Osbournes' pets are as devilishly fun as Jack's lovable bulldog, Lola. "She's so wonderfully sweet," says Melinda. No one's going to argue that point. But from the moment the Osbournes moved into their new home, Lola was a one-dog wrecking crew. "She's just the cutest thing," says Sharon. "But she ate and pooped her way through the first season."

Indeed, she was the inspiration behind some of Ozzy's most hilarious moments on the show. "It's like #$&*ing Dr. Doolittle's #$&*ing house here," he said upon walking in one day. Then he saw some dog poop on the floor, followed by a dog's bark, and he instantly knew the culprit.

"Lola!"

It happened repeatedly. If Lola wasn't laying land mines throughout the house, she was chewing the furniture and throwing it up. Jack explained that Lola was dysfunctional, but that didn't stop her misbehavior. Maybe nothing could. "Basically, she was a big dog in a little dog world," says Melinda. "She saw all those little dogs climbing onto the sofa and she'd want to get up there too. But she'd knock everything down in the process."

Lola was such a problem, they wondered if there was a boo
camp for dogs. Perhaps, but Sharon booked a professional do
trainer, which set off Ozzy. "No darling, you don't need a ther
apist," he scoffed. "You just need to get up at seven and ope
the #$&*ing door."

Enter Tamar Geller, a former Israeli army intelligence office
"When I walked in I was floored by how many dogs they had,
she remembers. "It was dogs everywhere. It was a happy situ
ation. But where would I look first?"

Easy. The rambunctious bulldog. Tamar guessed that Lola wa
spoiled rotten. Ozzy suggested that she was mad. Tamar called he
gorgeous and cute. "She's destructive," countered Ozzy. "Sh
jumps on my son's bed and urinates."

"I need *you* to make you more important in your dog's mind," she said

"Why don't we get a piece of wood and whack the dog 'round th
back of the head?" replied Ozzy.

Although Lola did splendidly in her training session, a twelve o
a scale of one to ten according to Tamar, the dog was soon bac
to her old habits. And Ozzy couldn't stand it. "She demolishes m
bed. She chews my furniture. Don't get me wrong, I love Lola
What I don't like is picking...I don't mind a #$&*ing Pomerania
turd, but when they're #$&*ing bulldog loads you got to get a
earthmover and a #$&*ing gasmask to go in the kitchen. It's lik
#$&*ing plutonium turds."

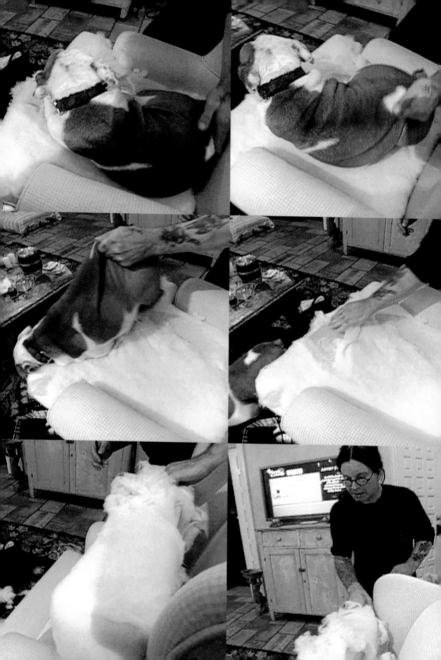

As a result, Sharon found Lola a new home with friends who brought her by for daily visits. Kelly liked the arrangement. "She's the cutest dog, but I don't miss stepping in her #$&*," she says. Jack was upset. "I don't feel like I was properly consulted," he says. "You shouldn't just be giving someone's dog away."

By fall, Lola was back home, and everyone seemed okay with her return—even after she devoured Sharon's latest purchase. "I bought some lovely new cushions with beads on them, and Lola proceeded to eat all the beads," says Sharon. "Oh well. She tries to change, but the poor darling can't get it. At least she's pooping outside."

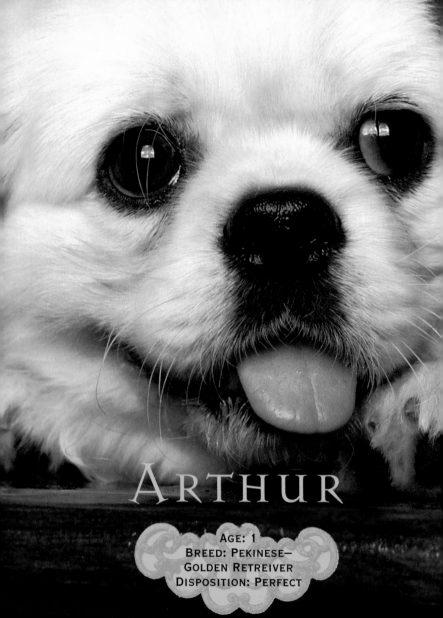

ARTHUR

AGE: 1
BREED: PEKINESE—
GOLDEN RETREIVER
DISPOSITION: PERFECT

"**A**rthur's kind of cool," says Jack of the Osbourne's newest dog who has, since his arrival in June, charmed his way into the hearts of the household. "I love Arthur," says Kelly. "I really, really love him."

And Ozzy's take? "Who's Arthur? Which one is he?"

Forgive Ozzy. He was on tour when Sharon brought Arthur home. She wasn't intending on buying a new dog, but she couldn't resist after stopping in the pet shop. "There was the cutest little dog," she says. "I picked him up and I'm like, 'What's this dog?' They go, 'He's a show Pekinese.'

"Well, I would have never gone out to buy a Pekinese, but they were going on about how incredibly perfect this one was. In truth, he was so loveable. He's made of rubber. You can put him in any way and he stays."

Bottom line: Sharon fell in love and brought him home. From day one, Arthur fit in with the family, hanging out in the kitchen, sleeping near Minnie and Maggie. He even weaseled his way into lying close to Sharon. But something about him struck her as peculiar. "I kept looking at him and I got all my dog

books out because he looked nothing like a Pekinese," says Sharon.

Instead of a squishy snout and long hair, he had a long nose and curly hair. Wanting a professional opinion, Sharon took him to the vet, who determined he was part Golden Retreiver. "That explained it," says Sharon. So he's part big dog, with the stubby little legs of a toy. "He reminds me of Toulouse–Lautrec," she says.

Since his TV debut on MTV's 2002 Video Music Awards, there's no doubt Arthur's made an impression. "If you ask me," says Kelly, "Arthur rules."

Chicken

Age: 7 months
Breed: Maltese
Disposition: A walking miracle

The good life did not come easily to this little dog. She was only a couple weeks old when Kelly spotted her in the window of a Beverly Hills pet store. Not only was she the runt of a litter of newborn Maltese pups, but she was very obviously sick. "She didn't have any hair, she was extremely thin, and just looked like crap," says Kelly, who nonetheless felt a stirring in her heart upon seeing the dog and took it home.

"I was talking to Sharon when she brought it inside," says Melinda, "and I said, 'Get that thing away from me.'" Sharon ordered her to take it to the animal hospital immediately. The vet who takes care of the family's other pets informed Kelly that this new addition—who she referred to simply as "this little thing"—probably wasn't going to survive long enough for her to think of a real name.

"What *wasn't* wrong with that poor thing?" says Melinda. "She had liver and stomach problems. A hernia. Hypoglycemia. Honestly, everything about her was a nightmare. I really couldn't stand to look at her. She made me too sad."

A week later, Kelly went to New York to start work on her record. She was accompanied by Sharon, Jack, Melinda, and...Chicken. "I was so upset," says Melinda,

who, as she predicted, got stuck caring for the dog while everyone else went about their business. "I thought, Oh #$&*, I'm going to be with this dog the whole time and it's just going to piss, #$&*, and vomit until it dies.'"

Fortunately, the opposite happened. Left to care for Chicken by herself in New York City after the Osbournes abruptly returned to LA to take care of a family crisis, Melinda took the dog to a Park Avenue vet. Chicken had a bunch of tests done, and then, as she says, "started feeding it."

"I don't know much about dogs," she adds, "but I know lots about babies and I just started treating it like a baby. I fed her with a spoon, wrapped her in a blanket, and took her everywhere I went. Gradually she got better."

Indeed, as Sharon says, "Chicken is like a real dog now." "But Melinda absolutely ruined her," says Kelly. Melinda doesn't deny the charge. Nor could she, considering Chicken sits on her shoulder while she types, curls up in her lap when she isn't working, rides with her to photo shoots, and is basically in love with the women who saved her life. And Melinda feels the same. "I'm obsessed by Chicken," she says. "I truly love that little dog. She's a miracle."

Lost Cat
MISSING
MOE
Egyptian black cat,
Skinny, Chisled face
Age 3, 10 lbs.
$ REWARD $

III

Cool Cats

ISTORY HAS PROVIDED
no shortage of edifying comments about cats
from great thinkers, including among others
Mark Twain ("If man could be crossed with a
cat, it would improve man, but it would deteri-
orate the cat"), Leonardo Da Vinci ("The smallest feline is a
masterpiece"), Miguel de Cervantes ("In the night all cats are
gray"), and Colette ("There are no ordinary cats"). Ozzy added a
classic remark of his own when he said, "The Osbourne family is
a great family of wasting money and saying, 'Well, maybe we
have too many dogs and so we'll throw the cats in just for fun.'"

"Oh, that's just Ozzy," says Sharon. "He might complain, but in
the end he knows all of us have so much love to give that it
would be unfair to not include a few cats." In fairness to Ozzy,
they've got more than a few. Let's meet 'em.

DIRTY
OLD GUS

A big, fat, slow-moving Rag Doll, a breed known for its long hair and deep affection for humans, he's always covered in leaves and kitty litter. His luxurious surroundings notwithstanding, he spends most days sitting outside in the dampest and dirtiest spot he can find, or else he snoozes in the kitchen sink. He doesn't mind if it's filled with dishes. In fact, the bigger the mess the more he likes it. Hence his name, Dirty Old Gus.

Puss

Don't try touching Puss. Rag Dolls are among the most affectionate of any breed of cat, but don't expect affection from this one. Puss is a terribly finicky girl. Although she looks cuddly, she is snooty, superior and won't have anything to do with any of the Osbournes, their pets, or anyone else—other than Sharon. She spends all day following Mrs. O., padding softly a few steps behind her. If Sharon gets up, so does Puss. In another life, she might have been a groupie. As long as she's in the same room as Sharon, she's purrfect.

TIGGER

Tigger is an Abyssinian, one of the oldest known breeds of cats. Elegant and incredibly smart, Abyssinians are terrific cats known for their friendliness to people. As the Osbournes know, Tigger is all that as well as a little peculiar. Notorious for hiding in the flowerpots, Tigger has a habit of pouncing on the ladies working around the house, particularly the maid, who has extremely long hair. Tigger likes jumping on her and getting tangled in her tresses. If you're at the Osbourne's and hear someone scream, your best bet is that Tigger has struck again.

HILLS

The latest addition to the Osbourne's menagerie, this pure black stray had the good fortune to be rescued by Sharon. She was visiting her brother, David, at the Beverly Hills Hotel one beautiful summer day when she heard the pained whining and screaming of an animal coming from somewhere nearby. Turning to the valets, she asked, "Where's the cat?"

Shrugging, they said the noises had been like that for the past two days. "And you haven't done anything?" asked Sharon. She immediately sent one valet to get a box, and when he came back, Sharon led him and several others into the flower bed until they found and caught the abandoned kitty. "I'm calling her Hills," she announced, "after the hotel."

Now Hills is best friends with Tigger. The two are virtually inseparable. They even sleep together. "I like to think Hills was waiting at the hotel for me," says Sharon.

Lost Cat!
MISSING:
MOE
Egyptian black cat,
Skinny, Chisled face,
Age 3, 10 lbs.
$ REWARD $

ꟿOE

Loved as much as any of the Osbourne's pets, Moe's story is a real cat-astrophe. An Egyptian black cat, he was very skinny with a chiseled faced. He looked as if he'd been sculpted from stone. He had a special air that led them to believe he'd been reincarnated from an ancient king or prince.

Then one day Moe disappeared. An all-out search determined the cat was missing. The Osbournes put up MISSING signs throughout Beverly Hills and notified the police. Over the ensuing days, they religiously called the station and checked with the pound. But he didn't turn up.

About four weeks later, Sharon and her kids returned to the shop where they had bought Moe, hoping to find another one like him. Instead the owner told them that someone had their cat. "How'd they know it was mine?" asked Sharon.

Apparently this family had been passing by the store when another Egyptian in the window caught their attention because they had just found an identical cat in their Beverly Hills neighborhood. Right away, the shop owner said, "That's Ozzy's cat!"

"Ozzy's cat?" they asked.

"Yeah, *the* Ozzy Osbourne," said the owner, who explained the story.

It turned out the family had picked the cat up from the street and brought it into their home, thinking it was starving. They didn't know Egyptian cats are naturally thin. Much to Sharon's disappointment, though, they no longer had the cat. As it turned out, when Moe didn't get along with their other pets, they gave him to their housekeeper. A few days later, their housekeeper gave him to a rescue organization and then the rescue group found him another home.

Which was all well and good–intentioned, but Sharon wanted their cat back. Yet the rescue group wouldn't tell her where they placed Moe. "And every time I call this cat place, they tell me to #$&* off," she says. "We've had our lawyer send them a letter, but we really need Ace Ventura, the pet detective, to bring back Moe."

"What can I say? They know they can #$&* and piss all over everything and I'm like, 'Okay, that's fine, darling. I'll clean it up.'"

— *Sharon*